HEINEMANN STATE STUDIES

Uniquely Connecticut

Phyllis Goldstein

Heinemann Library
Chicago, Illinois

Designed by Heinemann Library
Printed and bound in the United States,
North Mankato, Minnesota.

10
10 9 8 7 6 5 4 3

**Library of Congress
Cataloging-in-Publication Data**

Phyllis Goldstein.
  Uniquely Connecticut / Phyllis Goldstein.
     p. cm.—(Heinemann state studies)
Summary: Provides an overview of various aspects
of Connecticut that make it a unique state,
including its people, land, government, culture,
economy, and attractions.
Includes bibliographical references and index.
  ISBN: 978-1-4034-4488-2 (1-4034-4488-9) (HC)
  ISBN: 978-1-4034-4503-2 (1-4034-4503-6) (PBK)
  1. Connecticut--Juvenile literature. [1. Connecti-
cut] I. Title. II. Series.
  F776.3.B64 2003
  978.8—dc21
                                        2003009430

005664RP
022010

Cover Pictures

Main *Ship in Mystic Seaport*
Top (left to right) *Yale Univeristy, Connecticut
state flag, Nathan Hale, Connecticut farm*

Acknowledgments
Development and photo research by BOOK
BUILDERS LLC

The author and publishers are grateful to the following for permission to reproduce copyrighted
material:

Cover photographs by (top, L-R) Robert
Holmes/Corbis; Phil Schermeister/Corbis;
Bettmann/Corbis; Robin Prange/Corbis; (main)
Todd Gipstein/Corbis

Title page (L-R) Reuters New Media Inc./Corbis;
David Muench/Corbis; Joseph Sohm/Alamy
Images; contents page, 13B Bob Cranston/Animals
Animals; p. 5 Robert Homes/Corbis; p. 6 David
Muench/Corbis; pp. 7, 39, 45 International Map-
ping Associates; pp. 9T, 14M, 14B, 16, 19, 20B, 32,
38 Bettmann/Corbis; pp. 9B, 15, 43B, 44 Wendy
Carlson; pp. 11T, 24 Joseph Sohm/Alamy Images;
p. 13T Andre Jenny/Alamy Images; p. 13M
Michael P. Gadomski/Photo Researchers Inc.;
p. 14T Rod Planck/Photo Researchers Inc.; p. 17
Burstein Collection/Corbis; p. 18 Alamy Images;
p. 20T Najlah Feanny/Corbis SABA; p. 21 Corbis;
p. 22 Lichtenstein Andrew/Corbis SYGMA; p. 24
Joseph Sohm/Alamy Images; p. 25 printed with
permission of the Connecticut Judicial Branch;
p. 26 The Corcoran Gallery of Art/Corbis; p. 27 Lee
Snider/Corbis; pp. 28, 36 Phil Schermeister/
Corbis; p. 29 Raymond Gehman/Corbis; p. 30
Andrew J. Martinez/Photo Researchers Inc.; p. 31
R. Capozzelli/Heinemann Library; p. 34 Reuters
NewMedia Inc./Corbis; p. 35 Robin Prange/Corbis;
p. 37 Courtesy of Sikorsky Helicopter; p. 40T
Joseph Sohm; ChromoSohm Inc./Corbis; p. 40B
Todd Gipstein/Corbis; p. 42 Courtesy the Harriet
Beecher Stowe Center; p. 43T Courtesy the New
England Carousel Museum

Special thanks to Marcia H. Miner of the Fairfield
Historical Society for her expert comments in the
preparation of this book.

Every effort has been made to contact copyright
holders of any material reproduced in this book.
Any omissions will be rectified in subsequent
printings if notice is given to the publisher.

Some words are shown in bold, **like this.**
You can find out what they mean by looking
in the glossary.

Contents

Uniquely Connecticut

Connecticut is one of six New England states located in the northeast corner of the United States. All six were settled in the 1600s by people from England. Although Connecticut has much in common with other New England states, it is unique—a one-of-a-kind place. Connecticut's uniqueness lies in its many surprises.

Nearly two-thirds of Connecticut is open land, forests, and farms. Yet its cities and **suburbs** are among the nation's leading producers of machine tools, helicopters, jet engines, and submarines.

Connecticut is small in size. Only Delaware and Rhode Island have less land. Yet it also has more people than many bigger states. Its population is larger than that of North Dakota, South Dakota, Wyoming, and Montana combined. Connecticut's 3.4 million people are not scattered evenly across the state. About nine out of every ten people live along the coast or in the Connecticut River Valley.

ORIGINS OF THE STATE'S NAME

Native Americans, the first people to live in what is now Connecticut, named the land "Quinatucquet," which means "Beside the Long River." In the 1600s Europeans adopted the Native American name for the river and the land. They called both "Connecticut."

MAJOR CITIES

Connecticut's three largest cities are Hartford, New Haven, and Bridgeport. Hartford, the state's oldest city and its capital, is located on the Connecticut River. The Dutch and later the English established settlements there in the 1630s. Hartford soon became a center of trade and of farming. By 1638 it was also a center of government. It was the capital of Connecticut Colony.

Yale University was founded in 1701. From 1702 to 1707, classes were held in Milford and Saybrook before the school moved to New Haven in 1716.

Today Hartford is known as the **insurance** capital of the United States. By the early 1800s companies there were protecting **merchants** from losses due to fire, pirates, and accidents. Today the city is home to more than 50 insurance companies.

New Haven is a port on Long Island Sound. By the early 1800s, it had become a shipbuilding center and later in the century a factory town. Today the city is best known as the home of Yale University, the nation's third oldest university.

Bridgeport, the state's largest city, is named for the first drawbridge over the Poquonock River. The river and Bridgeport's deep harbor attracted merchants and shipbuilders in the 1700s. By the early 1800s people were also building factories there. By the 1930s the city had nearly 500. Although many are gone, Bridgeport is still a major producer of electrical equipment and other industrial products.

Connecticut's Geography and Climate

No part of Connecticut is more than a two-hour drive from Long Island Sound. The **sound** shapes the land and the climate of the state.

LAND

Geographers divide Connecticut into five regions. The Taconic Mountains in the northwest corner of the state have steep granite slopes and narrow valleys. The highest peaks in Connecticut are found there. The tallest is Bear Mountain, which stands 2,355 feet above sea level.

The Western Upland covers much of western Connecticut. Steep hills that average between 1,000 and 1,400 feet above sea level mark the region. The Eastern Upland is lower in **elevation,** with hills under 1,200 feet high. The Connecticut River Valley divides the two uplands and is about 25 to 35 miles wide in Connecticut. The land in the valley is a **plain** that contains Connecticut's most fertile farmland.

Every fall, the trees that cover the Litchfield Hills in the Western Upland turn yellow, red, and orange.

Hartford

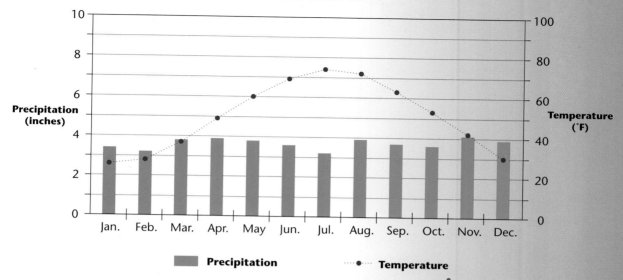

The Coastal Plain is a lowland about six to sixteen miles wide along Connecticut's southern border. The land is broken by bays, inlets, and the mouths of rivers.

CLIMATE

Climate is the usual weather of a place. How hot or cold the weather tends to be at various times in the year is part of the climate. So is how much **precipitation** a place gets. Wind, large bodies of water, and elevation also affect climate.

The Taconic Mountains have the highest elevation in Connecticut and the coldest temperatures. Air cools as it rises. So temperatures in the mountains are often 10°F cooler than lower land nearby.

The Coastal Plain is usually five to ten degrees warmer in winter and cooler in the summer than other parts of the state. Ocean breezes affect temperatures along the coast. Water heats up and cools off more slowly than land. As winds blow across Long Island Sound, they are warmed by the water in winter and cooled in summer.

Although precipitation does not vary much throughout the state, the mountains in the northwest get more snow than the rest of the state.

On average, Connecticut receives about 47 inches of precipitation a year.

Famous Firsts

INVENTED IN CONNECTICUT

David Bushnell of Old Saybrook invented the world's first submarine, the *American Turtle,* in 1775. It could stay underwater for 30 minutes.

Elias Howe patented his lockstitch sewing machine on September 10, 1846, in New Hartford.

Just two years after the telephone was invented in 1876, George C. Coy set up the world's first telephone network in New Haven. When it opened January 28, 1878, it had 21 subscribers. Around ten weeks later, Coy introduced the first telephone book, which had 50 names.

In 1932 Edwin Herbert Land of Bridgeport invented a coating that eliminated glare from glass and other shiny surfaces. In 1937 his Polaroid Corporation used that coating on sunglasses, camera filters, and headlights. In

To make the submarine go underwater, a seaman let water into the hull. To return to the surface, he pumped the water out.

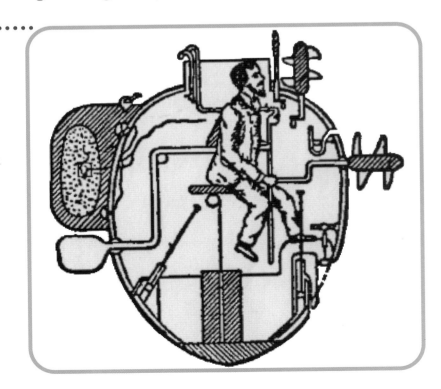

1947 he invented the first camera to take instant black-and-white photos and, in 1963, instant color photos.

Igor Sikorsky built the first helicopter in Stratford in 1939.

Igor Sikorsky pilots the helicopter he invented on its first flight in 1939.

LIBRARIES AND SCHOOLS

In 1656 North America's first public library opened in New Haven.

The nation's first children's library opened in 1803, in Salisbury. Known as the Scoville Memorial Library, it was also the first library built and supported by taxpayers.

In 1784 Tapping Reeve built a classroom next to his home. It became the Tapping Reeve Law School—the first in the nation. Today it is known as the Litchfield Law School.

Some graduates of Tapping Reeve's one-room law school went on to serve as governors, members of the U.S. Congress, and justices of the Supreme Court.

BOOKS AND NEWSPAPERS

The *Hartford Courant* is the nation's oldest newspaper still in print today. Printer Thomas Green started the newspaper in 1764.

In 1796 Amelia Simmons of Hartford published *American Cookery*, the first cookbook written in the United States. It contained recipes for pumpkin pudding, turtle soup, and other American dishes.

In 1828 Noah Webster published the first American dictionary. Its 70,000 words were spelled the American way rather than the English way (for example, *color* instead of *colour* and *music* instead of *musick*).

FOR THE FUN OF IT

In 1920 students at Yale University in New Haven accidentally invented the Frisbee. After lunch, they would toss around empty tin pie plates from the Frisbie Pie Company in Bridgeport. They yelled "Frisbee!" to warn passersby to look out for the flying plates.

In 1949 James Wright of New Haven invented Silly Putty, delighting children for generations to come.

In 1953 David Nelson Mullany of Shelton invented the wiffle ball, a plastic ball that curves when thrown.

A School for the Hearing Impaired

In the early 1800s many people thought that children who were hearing impaired could not learn. After watching a neighbor's child at play, Thomas Gallaudet of Hartford became convinced that they were wrong. The child, who lost her hearing as a baby, was Alice Cogswell. Gallaudet persuaded her father and a few others to start the American School for the Deaf, the first free school for hearing-impaired students in the nation. When it opened on April 15, 1817, Alice Cogswell was among its first students.

Connecticut's State Symbols

CONNECTICUT STATE FLAG

Connecticut adopted its state flag in 1897. The three grapevines on the shield stand for the three oldest settlements: Wethersfield (1635), Hartford (1636), and Windsor (1637).

During the Revolutionary War (1775–1783), Connecticut troops marched into battle under a flag much like the one that flies over the state today.

CONNECTICUT STATE SEAL

Connecticut's seal is based on the seal of the Saybrook Colony. In 1644 Saybrook became part of the Connecticut Colony and its seal became the seal of the Connecticut Colony.

When Connecticut declared its independence from Great Britain in 1776, lawmakers changed the "Colony of Connecticut" to the "Republic of Connecticut."

A Yankee Doodle Dandy

The British used words such as *dandy* and *macaroni* to describe men who dressed in the height of fashion. However, a "Yankee Doodle Dandy" was no fashion plate. The name was coined in 1756 to describe young volunteers from Connecticut who joined the British in a fight against the French and their Native American **allies** in the West.

STATE MOTTO: QUI TRANSTULIT SUSTINET

The state motto is Latin for "He Who Transplanted Still Sustains." The **colonists** believed that God had "transplanted" them from England to North America, where He continued to **sustain** them.

STATE NICKNAME: CONSTITUTION STATE

Although Connecticut has many nicknames, the official one chosen in 1959 is the "Constitution State." Many believe that Connecticut Colony had the first written **constitution.** Many of its features were later included in the U.S. Constitution.

STATE SONG: "YANKEE DOODLE"

The state song is "Yankee Doodle." Anyone from Connecticut and later New England was originally called a **Yankee.** The song became the rallying song for American troops during the **Revolutionary War** (1775–1783) and for the Union Army during the **Civil War** (1861–1865).

"Yankee Doodle"

Yankee Doodle went to town,
Riding on a pony,
Stuck a feather in his hat,
And called it macaroni.

Chorus
Yankee Doodle keep it up,
Yankee Doodle dandy,
Mind the music and the step,
And with the folks be handy.

State Flower: Mountain Laurel

The mountain laurel became the state flower in 1907. The plant, which is native to New England, is a shrub with pink and white blossoms.

State Tree: White Oak

The white oak became the state tree in 1947. It was selected to honor a white oak that holds a special place in the state's history. That tree, known as the **Charter Oak,** has become a symbol of freedom for all Americans.

Native Americans made spoons and other eating utensils from the wood of the mountain laurel. Perhaps that is why they called the plant "spoonwood."

White oaks can grow up to 150 feet high.

State Animal: Sperm Whale

The Connecticut General Assembly chose the sperm whale as the state animal in 1975 to honor the state's whaling industry. In the middle of the 1800s, it was the second largest in the United States. At the time, people used the animal's thick layer of blubber or fat to make oil to light lamps.

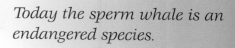

Today the sperm whale is an endangered species.

Europeans gave the American robin its name because its colors reminded them of those found on English robins.

. . . .

STATE BIRD: AMERICAN ROBIN

Connecticut adopted the American robin as its state bird in 1943. The American robin is really a **thrush** with a red breast and brown wings.

STATE HERO: NATHAN HALE

Nathan Hale of Coventry was a spy for the Americans during the Revolutionary War (1775–1783). When the British discovered what he was doing, they sentenced him to death without a trial. His last words have become famous: "I only regret that I have but one life to lose for my country." Hale inspired others to make sacrifices for their country. In 1985 Hale became the state's hero.

Nathan Hale was a teacher before he became a captain in Washington's army.

. . . .

. . . .

In 1886 Connecticut granted Prudence Crandall an annual pension of $400.

STATE HEROINE: PRUDENCE CRANDALL

Prudence Crandall opened the first school for African American women in New England in Canterbury in 1833. Angry townspeople repeatedly attacked the school and in 1834 the state made it a crime to educate African Americans without the approval of the town in which the school is located. Crandall was tried twice for breaking that law. She had to close her school due to a lack of funds. In 1995 she was voted "state heroine."

CONNECTICUT'S STATE QUARTER

In 1999 the U.S. government minted Connecticut's commemorative quarter. The design features Connecticut's state tree, the Charter Oak.

Connecticut's History and People

People have been living in what is now Connecticut for thousands of years. Until the 1600s nearly all of them were Native Americans.

NATIVE AMERICANS AND EUROPEAN SETTLERS

In 1633 Dutch traders set up a small post on the Connecticut River so they could trade for furs with Native Americans, such as the Pequot and Algonquin. These peoples lived by hunting, gathering, and fishing. They also grew corn, pumpkins, beans, and squash.

In 1635 new settlers began to arrive in Connecticut from Massachusetts. They came mainly in search of farmland. John Oldham, an English trader, established Wethersfield in 1635. The Reverend Thomas Hooker founded Hartford in 1636, and the Reverend John Warham started Windsor in 1637. All three settlements were located in the fertile Connecticut River Valley.

The Institute for American Indian Studies in Washington, Connecticut, has recreated an Algonquin village to show how Native Americans lived in the 1600s.

The Reverend Thomas Hooker led his congregation from what is now Cambridge, Massachusetts, to the Connecticut River Valley in 1638.

THE PEQUOT WAR

The Pequots were the only Native Americans to openly resist the newcomers. As the **colonists** and the Pequot quarreled over land, there were acts of violence on both sides. After the colonists killed a Pequot sachem or chief, the Pequot took revenge by murdering several colonists in 1636.

In the spring of 1637 a few hundred colonists under the command of Captain John Mason attacked the Pequots' main settlement at Mystic. The colonists killed more than 600 men, women, and children—more than half of the tribe's population. The war severely weakened the Pequot nation and gave the colonists control of the Connecticut River Valley.

THE FUNDAMENTAL ORDERS

Until 1638 Massachusetts ruled the Connecticut River Valley. That year, settlements there organized their own independent colony. To provide a government, the leaders of settlements in Connecticut created a document known as the Fundamental Orders. It was based on the idea that a government gets its right to rule from the people. Therefore, the people ought to elect their own leaders. The right to vote in the Connecticut Colony, however, was limited to men who owned property and belonged to the **Puritan** Church.

Also in 1638 two British **merchants,** John Davenport and Theophilus Eaton, founded New Haven Colony. Other settlements followed. These settlements centered on New Haven in much the way the Connecticut Colony centered on Hartford.

In 1658 England crowned a new king, Charles II. When colonists in Connecticut heard the news, many were

The Charter Oak

When James II became king of England in 1687, he united New York and the New England colonies under one government. He named Sir Edmund Andros governor. Andros demanded that Connecticut give up its charter. According to legend, when Andros came to seize the charter, someone knocked over the candles in the room. When the lights were lit again, the charter had disappeared. Someone hid it in an old white oak tree, later known as the Charter Oak. Nevertheless, Connecticut became part of the new colony. And so it remained until 1689, the year the British forced James II to leave his throne. Later that year, a new king restored the old colonial charters, including the one for Connecticut.

alarmed. Neither their colony nor the one at New Haven had a royal charter—a document issued by the king that defined the boundaries of the colony and its rights. In 1661 John Winthrop Jr., Connecticut's governor, persuaded the king to grant Connecticut a charter based on the Fundamental Orders. That charter also gave Connecticut control of the New Haven Colony. The two colonies were united in 1664.

THE REVOLUTIONARY WAR

In July 1776 thirteen British colonies along the north Atlantic declared their independence. Fighting between the colonists and the British had started earlier in 1775 and would continue until 1781. More than 40,000 men from Connecticut served in the Continental army, which is what the American side was called. Local residents supplied soldiers with so much gunpowder, food, and other goods that Connecticut became known as the Provisions State.

Although few battles were fought in Connecticut, the British burned Danbury in 1777 and Fairfield in 1779. Other towns were **looted.** In September 1781 British troops under the command of **traitor** Benedict Arnold captured Fort Griswold and burned New London.

THE CONNECTICUT COMPROMISE

During the war, Americans began to organize a national government. Their first effort was the Articles of Confederation. It went into effect in 1781. The government written up in the Articles, however, lacked an **executive branch.** When the new government proved to be too weak to defend the nation, **delegates** from almost every state met in Philadelphia in 1787 to write a new **constitution.**

Roger Sherman was the only man to sign the Declaration of Independence, the Articles of Association, the Articles of Confederation, and the Constitution.

At one point, the delegates were deadlocked. They could not decide how many representatives each state should have in the U.S. Congress. Roger Sherman of Connecticut offered a **compromise.** He suggested that Congress be divided into two houses: the Senate and the House of Representatives. To satisfy the less populous states, every state would have two senators. However, the number of representatives from each state would be based on its population. The more populous the state, the more representatives it would have.

The compromise ended the deadlock. In 1788 Connecticut became the fifth state to **ratify** the U.S. Constitution.

CONNECTICUT IN A NEW NATION

In the late 1700s and early 1800s Connecticut became an industrial center. After the **Civil War** (1861–1865), manufacturing grew faster than ever. Every town seemed to have a specialty. Danbury was known for its hats, Bristol for its clocks, and Meriden for its silverware. New Britain became the "hardware city" and Waterbury the "brass city." As the economy expanded, Connecticut attracted many **immigrants.** By 1910 one out of every three people in Connecticut was foreign born. Most were from Ireland, Italy, Russia, Germany, and Austria. Today Connecticut is home to 3.4 million people. About eight out of every ten people live in urban areas.

FAMOUS PEOPLE

Katharine Hepburn (1907–2003), film star. Hepburn was born in Hartford. She won four Academy Awards for Best Actress in a Leading Role.

Governor Ella Grasso won reelection as governor in 1978.

Ella Tambussi Grasso (1919–1981), politician. The daughter of Italian immigrants, Ella Tambussi was born in Windsor Locks. She served in the Connecticut House of Representatives from 1953 to 1957. From 1958 to 1970 she was Connecticut's secretary of state and from 1970 to 1974 a member of the U.S. Congress. In 1974 she became the first woman to be elected governor on her own.

Like his father and grandfather, George W. Bush is a graduate of Yale University in New Haven.

Previously, the nation's only women governors were elected to complete their husbands' terms if their husbands had died while in office.

Ralph Nader (1934–   ), consumer advocate. Born in Winsted, Nader graduated from Princeton University and Harvard Law School. While at Harvard, Nader learned that automakers were more interested in style than safety. In 1966 he launched a successful campaign for laws that would protect drivers and their passengers in the event of an accident. Since then, he has pressed for other laws that protect consumers and workers.

George W. Bush (1946–   ), president of the United States (2001–   ). Born in New Haven, Bush grew up in Texas. He served as governor of Texas from 1995 to 2001. Bush, whose father was president from 1989 to 1993, is the first son of a president to win the presidency since the election of John Quincy Adams in 1824.

Dorothy Hamill (1956–   ), ice skater. Born in Riverside, Hamill won the gold medal in figure skating at the 1976 Winter Olympics in Austria and the 1974 and 1976 world championships.

Dorothy Hamill receives the gold medal at the Winter Olympics in 1976.

Yankee Ingenuity

The word *ingenuity* means cleverness or creativity. **Yankees** have a reputation for being clever. In the early 1800s they developed new machines and new ways of working that changed the way people lived and worked. Those changes were so great that they are considered a revolution—the **Industrial Revolution** (1700s).

The American Industrial Revolution began in New England in the late 1700s. Connecticut played an important role. Eli Whitney of New Haven and Samuel Colt of Hartford were among those who changed the way goods were manufactured.

INTERCHANGEABLE PARTS

In the late 1700s Eli Whitney invented a new method for making goods. He got the idea after watching machines stamp out coins, each exactly like the next. He decided to apply that idea to the manufacture of rifles. In 1798 the U.S. government asked Whitney to make 10,000 weapons in two years at a cost of $13.48 for each weapon. Many people thought it was a joke. They said it was impossible to produce so many guns that quickly or cheaply.

At the time, a single **artisan** made every firearm. Each was unique. Its parts did not fit any other gun. Whitney's idea was to

Eli Whitney built his gun factory outside New Haven.

Manufacturers used interchangeable parts and assembly lines to produce ammunition, clocks, carriages, and other goods.

make all of the parts of his rifles the same. Whitney's system would dramatically reduce the time and money used to make goods.

Whitney did not fill the government order until 1809. He used that time to design the machines and other tools needed to make each part of the weapon interchangeable. Once he made 500 firearms, he showed President John Adams and Vice President Thomas Jefferson how his idea worked. He took apart ten weapons, mixed up the parts, and reassembled them within minutes. The men were astonished.

THE ASSEMBLY LINE

In 1835 Samuel Colt, a gun manufacturer from Hartford, took Whitney's idea a step further. He produced his firearms on an assembly line.

Colt divided the task of making a revolver among many workers. One made barrels, another triggers, and yet another assembled the parts. Working together, they could turn out more guns in less time than a skilled artisan working alone. By the late 1800s most American manufacturers were using the ideas of Whitney and Colt to turn out a variety of goods. Europeans called this method of production "the American system." It is still in use today in countries around the world.

Coltsville

By the 1840s a community had grown up around Samuel Colt's factory. Known as Coltsville, it became a center of **innovation** in much the same way that California's "Silicon Valley" was a center for innovation in computer technology in the late 1900s. It was in Coltsville where Samuel Morse came up with the idea of the telegraph in 1844. It was also in Coltsville in the 1950s where engineers developed the technology needed to build jet engines.

Connecticut's State Government

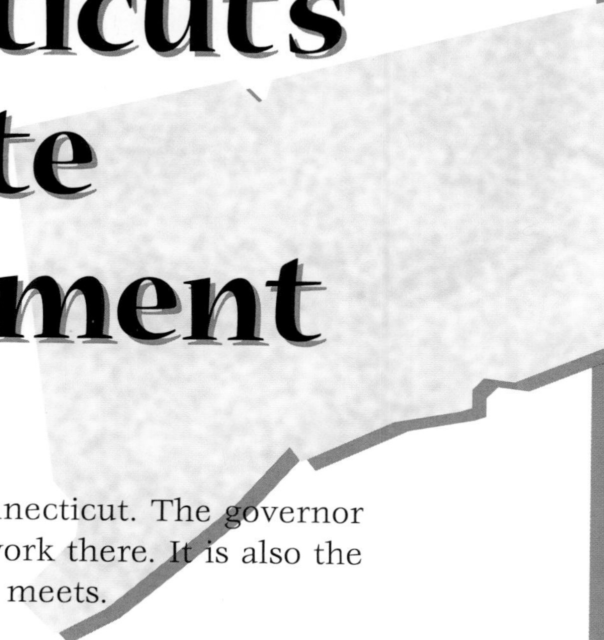

Hartford is the capital of Connecticut. The governor and many other state officials work there. It is also the place where the state legislature meets.

Connecticut's government is based on a **constitution,** which was adopted in 1965. It explains how the government is supposed to work. It also protects the rights and freedoms of the people of Connecticut. Among the

Executive Branch

Governor & Lt. Governor
(four-year term)

Carries out the laws of the state

Legislative Branch

General Assembly

House of Representatives 151 Representatives (two-year term)	Senate 36 Senators (four-year term)

Makes laws for the state

Judicial Branch

Supreme Court
7 Judges

Appeals Court
9 Appellate Judges

Lower Courts
Superior Courts 180 Judges
Probate Court 133 Judges

Explains laws

Hartford and New Haven were cocapitals or shared capitals of Connecticut for more than 170 years—from 1701 to 1875.

freedoms it protects are the right to free speech and a free press.

Connecticut's state government is organized much like the federal government. It, too, is divided into three branches: legislative, executive, and judicial.

LEGISLATIVE BRANCH

The General Assembly, Connecticut's legislature, is made up of two parts, a senate and a house of representatives. The state's voters elect 36 senators and 151 representatives every two years. These are the men and women who make the state's laws.

EXECUTIVE BRANCH

The executive branch is the part of government that enforces the state's laws and runs Connecticut from day to day. The governor heads this branch of government. The second-highest official is the lieutenant governor. The lieutenant governor takes the governor's place when he or she is out of the state or unable to work. Both officials serve a four-year term.

Also elected to four-year terms are the secretary of the state, the treasurer, the comptroller, and the attorney general. The secretary of the state keeps public records and manages state elections. The treasurer handles the state's money, while the comptroller pays the state's bills. The attorney general is the state's lawyer. He or she represents the state in court.

JUDICIAL BRANCH

The judicial branch is the part of the government that decides how a state law applies in a particular case. The judicial branch is made up of four different kinds of courts: probate courts, superior courts, **appellate** courts, and the state supreme court.

Probate judges are elected to a four-year term. The governor appoints all other judges from a list of qualified candidates. These judges serve eight-year terms. They can be renominated and reappointed. Connecticut's 133 probate courts mainly oversee the distribution of property left in **wills.**

Most legal disputes are heard in superior courts. The state's 180 superior court judges try criminal and civil cases. Robbery, murder, and fraud are examples of criminal cases. Disagreements that involve rental agreements, contracts, and property are examples of civil cases. If either side in a court case is dissatisfied with the decision reached by the superior court, he or she can ask Connecticut's appellate court to review the case. If these judges disagree with the superior court's decision, they can reverse or change it.

The highest court is the state supreme court. It consists of a chief justice and six associates. Like the appellate court, it is a court of appeals. It is the job of the state supreme court to decide if a law that has been challenged is constitutional—that is, in keeping with the state constitution.

The Connecticut Supreme Court hears cases between September and June.

Connecticut's Culture

Connecticut has made many contributions to the nation's cultural heritage. Those contributions include the visual arts and theater.

ART IN CONNECTICUT

In the late 1800s American artists helped develop a new style of painting. They made their work seem more lifelike by showing how light affects the way people, buildings, and objects look. For most of the year, these artists lived in Boston and New York City. During the summer, many traveled to towns such as Greenwich and Old Lyme to paint and escape the heat of the city.

Many artists stayed in Old Lyme. Some took classes from well-known painters like Childe Hassam and Henry Ward Ranger. Florence Griswold, a local woman, turned her home into a boarding house for the artists and her barn into studios. Among the artists who stayed at the Griswold mansion was Willard Metcalf.

Short of rent money, Metcalf offered Griswold *May Night,* a painting of her and her home. She

Metcalf's painting captures the way Florence Griswold and her home looked on a warm spring evening.

Boarding Houses and Boarders

The owner of a boarding house rents rooms and provides one or two meals a day to paying guests. The artists who came to Connecticut for the summer often stayed at boarding houses such as the Bush-Holley House in Cos Cob (shown here) or Florence Griswold's

home in Old Lyme. Today both houses are tourist attractions. People come to see the places that inspired famous artists.

refused to accept it because it was one of his best efforts. Today the painting hangs in the Corcoran Gallery of Art in Washington, D.C. His other works can be found in such museums as the Art Institute of Chicago and the Metropolitan Museum of Art in New York.

THEATER IN CONNECTICUT

Painters were not the only artists who spent their summers in Connecticut. Since the early 1900s, Connecticut has been a place where people in the theater often try out their ideas and experiment with new techniques before showing them to a large audience.

So many successful plays had their start at New Haven's Schubert Performing Arts Center that the theater is known as "the birthplace of the nation's hits." Perhaps the biggest hit was a 1943 **musical** called *Away We Go*. Created by Richard Rogers and Oscar Hammerstein II, it

The Goodspeed Opera House was built in 1876 for theatergoers. They came by train, carriage, and even steamship from as far away as New York City.

was the first American musical to fit songs to specific characters and the plot of the play. When it left New Haven for Broadway, the play had a new title—*Oklahoma!*

The Goodspeed Opera House in East Haddam is the only theater in the United States dedicated to preserving the heritage of the musical and developing new works. Fifteen musicals developed at Goodspeed have opened on Broadway, including *Annie* and *Man of La Mancha.*

Over the past 30 years, the Eugene O'Neill Memorial Theater Center's National Playwrights Conference in Waterford has supported more than 330 writers and produced nearly 500 plays. Among those who have studied at the theater are Michael Douglas, Kevin Kline, and Meryl Streep.

Connecticut's Food

Over the centuries Native Americans and European settlers have created a variety of dishes using foods native to Connecticut. Those foods include corn, squash, beans, a variety of berries, and maple syrup.

CONNECTICUT SHELLFISH

Shellfish have long been an important source of food in Connecticut. Over the years people have developed many ways of preparing them. For example, oysters can be eaten fried, broiled, boiled, and even raw. In the 1890s Connecticut had the world's largest fleet of oyster steamships in the world. Oyster fishers found customers for their oysters as far away as Japan. Today, Connecticut ranks first in the nation in the value of its oyster beds and second in the production of oysters.

Fishers such as these haul hundreds of pounds of oysters out of Long Island Sound.

Quahogs, a variety of a hard-shelled clams, are found in the waters of the Atlantic Ocean from Canada to North Carolina.

Connecticut's most famous dish is seafood chowder. A chowder is a thick, chunky soup usually made with fish, potatoes, and milk. Cooks often use lobster, clams, mussels, or crab in their chowders. The hot soup has been warming fishers coming in from the cold for centuries.

Seafood Chowder

Be sure to get the help of an adult for this and other recipes.

Ingredients

1½ pound cod fillets, fresh or frozen

¼ pound bacon, diced

1 medium onion, finely chopped

½ cup celery, diced

1 chicken bouillon cube

2 cups boiling water

2 cups potatoes, diced

1 teaspoon salt

¼ teaspoon thyme

1 cup evaporated milk

1 cup regular milk

If you are using frozen fillets, thaw them first. Fry bacon in a pot until crisp and brown. Remove the bacon but leave the fat in the pot. Sauté the onion and the celery in remaining fat until tender.

Boil the 2 cups of water and dissolve the chicken bouillon cube in the boiling water. Add this mix to the onions and celery. Then add the potatoes, salt, and thyme.

Cover and simmer until the potatoes are tender. While the soup is simmering, cut the fish into 1½-inch cubes. Add the chunks of fish and cook until tender.

After the fish is cooked, add the evaporated milk and regular milk. Slowly raise the heat to blend flavors, but do not boil or the chowder may burn.

Connecticut's Folklore and Legends

Legends and folklore are stories that are not totally true but are often based on bits of truth. The people of Connecticut have passed down many stories about their state from one generation to the next.

THE LEGEND OF THE BLACK DOG

Three mountains overlook Meriden in central Connecticut. For years, one of those mountains, the West Peak, has attracted many hikers, even though some of them have died mysteriously along its trails. When local residents hear of yet another death, they shake their heads and mutter, "It is the dog, again."

According to the stories the townspeople tell, the dog leaves no footprints. When it barks, there is no sound. And it is whispered, "If a person shall meet the black dog once, it shall be for joy; and if twice, it shall be for sorrow; and the third time, he or she shall die."

Those who question the saying are often told the story of W. H. C. Pynchon, who came to the area in 1898.

On one visit, he encountered a friendly black dog on the West Peak. On his next visit, Pynchon brought along a friend who had seen the dog twice before. That day, Pynchon's friend fell to his death.

A few years later, Pynchon died in almost the same spot where his friend had lost his life. Did Pynchon see the black dog? No one will ever know.

A TALL TALE ABOUT A TALL MAN

Ethan Allen (1738–1789) of Litchfield led a band of volunteers during the **Revolutionary War.** Known as the Green Mountain Boys (most were from the Green Mountains of Vermont), they captured Forts Ticonderoga and Crown Point in New York in 1775, a year before the war began. Those victories gave Americans confidence that they could defeat the British.

Allen became a hero. Even before his victories in the Revolutionary War, many stories were told about him. Allen stood six feet, six inches tall at a time when the average man was about five feet, six inches tall. He had a reputation for being tough and independent.

According to one story, Allen and his cousin fell asleep under a shady tree on a hot summer day. A strange noise woke his cousin. To his horror, he saw a rattlesnake bite Allen again and again. Before he could kill the snake, it slithered away. A few minutes later, Allen rose from his nap rested and ready to return to work, although he did complain about the "mosquitoes" that disturbed his rest.

Ethan Allen spent two years as a prisoner of war aboard British prison ships, in British prisons, and in the New York City Jail. The British released him in 1778.

Connecticut's Sports Teams

Connecticut is located midway between one of the nation's great baseball rivalries—between the New York Yankees and the Boston Red Sox. Generally, people in northern Connecticut are Red Sox fans and those in southern Connecticut are Yankee fans. Those divisions disappear when it is time to root for one of the state's own teams.

MINOR LEAGUE BASEBALL

Connecticut has four minor league baseball teams—the New Haven Ravens, the Bridgeport Bluefish, the Norwich Navigators, and the New Britain Rock Cats. New Britain has produced 121 major leaguers, including Roger Clemens, Mo Vaughn, and Jeff Bagwell.

Good-bye Hartford Whalers

The Hartford Whalers were Connecticut's first, and so far only, major league sports team. Created in 1972 and originally called the New England Whalers, the team played hockey for two years in Boston before moving to Hartford. The Whalers played eighteen seasons in Hartford, but they had only three winning seasons. The Whalers moved to Raleigh, North Carolina, in 1997 and became the Carolina Hurricanes. In 2002 the Hurricanes played for the National Hockey League's Stanley Cup.

COLLEGE BASKETBALL IN CONNECTICUT

The University of Connecticut (UConn) men's and women's basketball teams, both called the Huskies, have a dedicated following in Connecticut. In 2003 the women's team won its fourth National Collegiate Athletic Association (NCAA) women's basketball championship in ten years. From the start of the 2001–2002 season to the end of the 2002–2003 season, the women lost just 1 game and won a record-breaking 70 games in a row.

In 2003 the U.S. Basketball Writers Association named guard Diana Taurasi and coach Geno Auriemma national player and national coach of the year, respectively. Taurasi was also named the NCAA Player of the Year. She is the second consecutive UConn player to win the award for basketball. Sue Bird won the 2001–2002 award. In 1999 UConn's men's basketball team won its first NCAA championship. Richard Hamilton, who now plays for the NBA's Detroit Pistons, led the Huskies to the title.

UConn graduate Sue Bird was the top draft pick in the 2002 Women's National Basketball Association draft. She now plays for the Seattle Storm.

Connecticut's Businesses and Products

In the 1700s many people in Connecticut earned their living by farming. Others turned to the sea. By the early 1800s more and more people were finding jobs in factories that turned out a wide range of goods.

Today a few people in Connecticut still fish and farm, and manufacturing is still important in the state, however, most people in Connecticut work in **service industries.** They buy or sell goods, run offices, fix computers, provide health care, operate buses and trains, offer legal services, teach, and carry out dozens of other jobs that help people.

Most farmers in Connecticut today specialize. Most raise dairy cows, tobacco, poultry, or fruits and vegetables.

Built by the Travelers Insurance Company in 1919, the 527-foot Travelers Tower was New England's first skyscraper.

SERVICE INDUSTRIES

Connecticut's first major service industry was the **insurance** business. It began in Hartford in 1794 with the creation of the Hartford Fire Insurance Group. The Aetna Fire Insurance Company opened for business in 1819. In the years that followed, other companies were formed. Insurers in Connecticut were the first in the nation to offer accident, auto, and aviation policies. Today the state has more than 100 insurance companies.

Banks, hospitals, television and radio stations, and state and local governments also provide services. Each year, visitors to Connecticut spend about $5 billion in the state. They explore museums; hike in state parks; buy souvenirs; attend sporting events, concerts, and plays; eat in restaurants; and stay in hotels.

Many large corporations in other industries have their headquarters in Connecticut, too. Among them are General Electric, GTE, Xerox, Uniroyal, and United Technologies. Many are located in towns along the southeastern coast near New York City. These companies employ thousands of service workers to manage their businesses, keep records, pay bills, and sell products.

MANUFACTURING

Although manufacturers are no longer Connecticut's leading employers, factories are still an important source of wealth in the state. In the 1800s guns, sewing machines, and clocks were among the state's leading products. Today the state's leading product is transportation equipment. Workers in Connecticut make parts for automobiles and airplanes, build helicopters, and **assemble** submarines. For example, Pratt and Whitney's North Haven plant makes the blades used on jet engines.

In the late 1700s Connecticut provided George Washington's army with firearms and ammunition. Connecticut companies still produce products for the military. They are an important part of the nation's defense industry. The Colt Manufacturing Company, for example, makes ammunition, guns, and other weapons.

Sikorsky Aircraft, which is now part of United Technologies, builds helicopters for the armed forces. Its founder, Igor Sikorsky, made the first helicopter in 1939. Today, workers at the plant that bears his name turn out helicopters like the Black Hawk. The company also makes the Seahawk. The navy uses it to hunt submarines, target missiles, and carry out search-and-rescue missions. These aircraft are sold not only to the United States but also to 25 countries around the world, in-

Black Hawk helicopters have been used in combat and special operations, including during the war in Iraq in 2003.

cluding Argentina, Egypt, Israel, Malaysia, Spain, Thailand, and Turkey.

In 1910 the Electric Boat Company, which is now owned by General Dynamics, acquired a shipyard at Groton. It built the submarines the U.S. Navy used during **World War I** (1914–1919) and **World War II** (1941–1945). Groton is still a major center for the design, engineering, and assembly of submarines, including those powered by **nuclear energy.** In 1954 workers at the Groton shipyard launched the USS *Nautilus,* the world's first nuclear submarine.

On July 23, 1958, the Nautilus *became the first ship ever to cross the North Pole.*

Attractions and Landmarks

Connecticut has a variety of attractions and land-marks. Many of them date back to colonial times. Others highlight the state's environment, celebrate its cultural contributions, and honor its industries.

Places to see in Connecticut

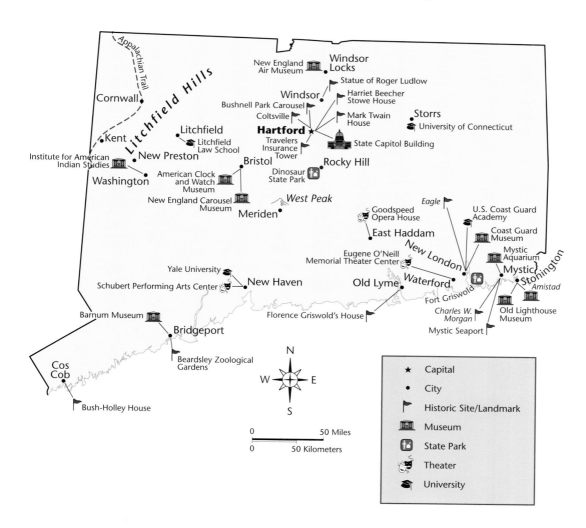

Legend:
- ★ Capital
- • City
- ⚑ Historic Site/Landmark
- 🏛 Museum
- State Park
- Theater
- University

When the lighthouse at Stonington was built in 1823, its 30-foot tower supported a lantern containing ten oil lamps with reflectors. The light they cast could be seen from twelve miles out at sea.

COASTAL ATTRACTIONS

Many people enjoy visiting Connecticut's thirteen **lighthouses** along its coastline. Today the Old Lighthouse Museum in Stonington on Connecticut's eastern shore recalls the years when dozens of lighthouses lined the New England coast.

The lighthouse in Stonington displays hundreds of artifacts of the whaling and fishing industries. Among them are models of ships as well as toys and ivory carvings. Sailors often made these objects to pass the time on long voyages. Visitors can also climb its long winding staircase to the top of the lighthouse—the place where the lighthouse keeper lit the lamps that guided whalers, fishing boats, and other ships safely to shore.

Mystic Seaport in Mystic draws about 465,000 visitors each year. Built in 1929 to look like a New England seaport in the early 1800s, it has a shipsmith shop, a sail loft, a one-room schoolhouse, a hardware store, and other buildings. Some of the buildings were brought from other parts of New England.

More than 200 old boats are docked in the Mystic Seaport.

Visitors to Mystic can climb aboard the many old ships in the harbor. Among those ships is a copy of the *Amistad*, a slave ship built in the 1830s.

In 1839 the *Amistad* was traveling from Havana, Cuba, to another part of the island when the 53 kidnapped Africans aboard took over the ship and ordered the crew to sail back to Africa. Instead, the sailors accidentally steered the ship toward the United States. The U.S. Navy intercepted it in Long Island Sound and brought the Africans to New Haven to stand trial for **mutiny.** Two years later, the Africans were set free and allowed to sail home. The replica of their ship now sails around the United States as a floating museum.

As its name suggests, the U.S. Coast Guard protects the nation's shoreline. Its agents fight oil spills, enforce immigration laws, ensure that ships pay taxes on goods brought into the United States, and conduct search-and-rescue missions. The first U.S. Coast Guard Academy opened in 1875 aboard the cutter ship *Dobbin.* In 1932 the academy moved ashore and built its current school in New London. The school still has its own training ship, the *Eagle.* If it is in port, visitors are welcome aboard. The nearby Coast Guard Museum has more than 200 model ships.

HISTORIC LANDMARKS AND MUSEUMS

In Washington, south of New Preston in the Litchfield Hills, is the Institute for American Indian Studies. The institute covers 10,000 years of Native American life in Connecticut with replicas of such dwellings as a prehistoric rock shelter and an Algonquin village and garden in the 1600s.

Mystic Aquarium

One of the highlights at Mystic Aquarium is the Beluga Whale exhibit. These small white whales look like dolphins. Other exhibits feature the colorful fish that live in warm waters off the coast of islands in the Pacific. Another exhibit showcases penguins, who waddle freely around their open tank.

The Barnum Museum in Bridgeport is dedicated to P. T. Barnum and his famous Ringling Brothers, Barnum and Bailey Circus. There is a model of the three-ring circus Barnum invented in 1881 and exhibits that showcase his best-known attractions. One of them was General Tom Thumb. Barnum claimed that at 28 inches tall, Thumb was the world's smallest man.

The Harriet Beecher Stowe Center features exhibits of Stowe's manuscripts, letters, and photographs.

Among the many historic places in Connecticut is the Harriet Beecher Stowe House in Hartford. It is the house where the author of *Uncle Tom's Cabin* lived at the end of her life. She moved there in 1873 and remained there until her death in 1896. Nearby is the Mark Twain House. It is the house where Samuel Clemens lived with his wife and children from 1873 until the 1890s. The home looks much the way it did when Clemens sat in his library and wrote *Tom Sawyer* in 1876.

Bristol was the center of the clock-making industry in Connecticut in the 1800s. Today some of the great clocks produced in the town are on display at the American Clock and Watch Museum. Clocks on display include a huge clock made entirely of wood—even its workings were carved from wood.

Bristol is also home to the New England Carousel Museum. It contains 300 pieces of carousel art, many of

The New England Carousel Museum runs the Bushnell Park Carousel in Hartford. Built in 1914, the merry-go-round contains 36 jumper horses, 12 stander horses, 2 chariots, and a Wurlitzer 153-band organ.

which were made by hand in the late 1800s and early 1900s.

The New England Air Museum is in Windsor Locks. It is one of only four large museums of aviation history in the United States. The oldest item in the museum is a wood-and-canvas monoplane built in 1909. There is also a collection of **World War II** (1941–1945) fighters and bombers and modern jets.

NATURE IN CONNECTICUT

The Appalachian Trail, a path that is more than 2,000 miles long, starts in Maine and continues south through fourteen states to Georgia. The trail is

Connecticut's part of the Appalachian trail rises in elevation from 260 feet to 2,316 feet above sea level.

one of the longest and most scenic hiking paths in the United States. About 56 miles of the trail run through Connecticut from Kent to Cornwall.

Dinosaur State Park in Rocky Hill has 2,000 dinosaur footprints. Scientists think those footprints are more than 200 million years old. The dinosaur tracks were accidentally discovered in 1966. A construction crew uncovered them while digging the foundation for a new government building. Five hundred of the tracks are now enclosed within an exhibit center. The rest are buried to keep them safe.

The Beardsley Zoological Gardens has been around for 81 years. The zoo contains more than 300 animals, including such **endangered species** as a Serbian tiger, a red wolf, and an andean condor. Other exhibits include a South American rain forest with a free-flight **aviary.**

About 250,000 people visit the Beardsley Zoological Gardens annually.

Map of Connecticut

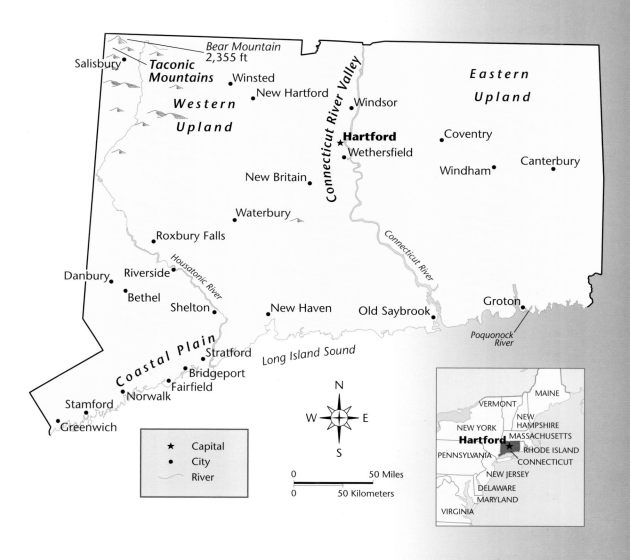

Salisbury

Taconic Mountains

Bear Mountain
2,355 ft

Western Upland

Winsted

New Hartford

Connecticut River Valley

Windsor

★ **Hartford**
Wethersfield

New Britain

Waterbury

Roxbury Falls

Eastern Upland

Coventry

Windham

Canterbury

Danbury

Riverside

Bethel

Shelton

Housatonic River

New Haven

Old Saybrook

Groton

Connecticut River

Poquonock River

Coastal Plain

Stratford

Bridgeport

Fairfield

Norwalk

Stamford

Greenwich

Long Island Sound

N
W · E
S

★ Capital
• City
⌇ River

0   50 Miles
0   50 Kilometers

MAINE
VERMONT
NEW YORK
NEW HAMPSHIRE
Hartford ★
MASSACHUSETTS
RHODE ISLAND
CONNECTICUT
PENNSYLVANIA
NEW JERSEY
DELAWARE
MARYLAND
VIRGINIA

Glossary

ally one who supports another

appellate having the power to hear or review appeals

artisan a skilled craftsperson who works mainly with hand tools

assemble to fit together the parts of a product

Charter Oak a white oak that has become a symbol of freedom for all Americans

Civil War (1861–1865) war between the Southern and Northern states over the issue of slavery

colonist a settler in a distant land that is ruled by his or her home country

compromise a settlement of a disagreement in which each side gives a little

constitution a plan that establishes the duties and limits of a government

delegate a representative to a convention

elevation height above sea level

endangered species a species of animal faced with extinction

executive branch the branch of government in charge of carrying out the laws of a state

immigrant a person who settles in a foreign country

Industrial Revolution a time beginning in the 1700s when more and more goods were made by machine rather than by hand

innovation a new idea

insurance the business of protecting people or property from losses as a result of fire, theft, or other dangers

lighthouse a tower topped by a powerful light that guides ships at sea

looted to have stolen goods

merchant one who buys and sells goods

musical a production that uses popular songs and dialogue to tell a story

mutiny open rebellion against authority

nuclear energy energy released by splitting atoms into tiny particles

plain an area of land that is flat or level

precipitation water that falls as rain or snow

Puritan member of a group of English Protestants in the 16th and 17th centuries who believed in strict religious discipline

ratify officially approve

Revolutionary War (1775–1783) the war for American independence between the colonists and the British

service industry a business that helps people in some way

sound a waterway that is usually connected to an ocean or other large body of water

suburb an area where people live, located near a city

sustain to maintain

thrush a songbird with brown feathers and a spotted breast

traitor a person who betrays his or her country, a cause, or trust

wills legal documents that tell how a person wishes to dispose of his or her possessions after death

World War I (1914–1919) a war in which Great Britain, the United States, and other allies defeated Germany and its allies

World War II (1941–1945) a war in which the U.S. and its allies defeated Germany, Italy, and Japan

Yankee a native of a northern state, particularly a New England state; a citizen of the United States

More Books to Read

• •

Bailer, Darice. *Connecticut: The Constitution State.* Milwaukee, Wis.: Gareth Stevens Publishing, 2002.

McNair, Sylvia. *Connecticut.* New York: Children's Press, 1999.

Murphy, Jim. *A Young Patriot: The American Revolution as Experienced by One Boy.* New York: Clarion, 1996.

Pell, Edward. *Connecticut.* Mankato, Minn.: Capstone Press, 2003.

Index

About the Author

Phyllis Goldstein is a former teacher and publisher who lives next door to Connecticut in Massachusetts. She is a writer and editor of books for young readers.